Clara Barton
The Angel of the Battlefield

by Theodore Stevenson

Cover, p.3, p.4, p.6, p.7, p.8, p.9, p.12, ©The Granger Collection, New York; p.5, p.10, p.11, p.13, ©Corbis; p.14, ©Library of Congress.

Printed in China

ISBN 10: 0-15-351442-6
ISBN 13: 978-0-15-351442-5

Ordering Options
ISBN 10: 0-15-351213-X (Grade 3 Advanced Collection)
ISBN 13: 978-0-15-351213-1 (Grade 3 Advanced Collection)
ISBN 10: 0-15-358077-1 (package of 5)
ISBN 13: 978-0-15-358077-2 (package of 5)

4 5 6 7 8 9 10 0940 12 11 10 09

Young Clara

Clara Barton was born on December 25, 1821. She was the youngest of five children. Clara was an excellent and talented student but very shy. When she was only seventeen years old, she became a teacher!

As a child, Clara had learned how to ride a horse and shoot a rifle. She preferred to play outside rather than stay in the house. She knew how to control a team of horses. Now, as an adult, she was both strong and smart.

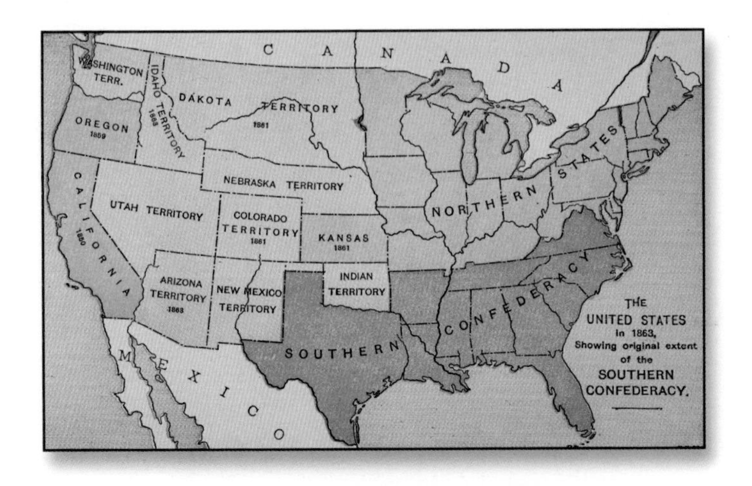

In 1861, the Civil War began. Clara hoped to serve her country by fighting for the Union. Clara had been raised in Massachusetts, and she supported the Union. The Union was the northern part of the United States. The Confederacy was the southern part. The Confederacy wanted to form its own country.

The Union wanted to keep the United States together. When the two sides could not agree, the Civil War began. Armies from the North and South battled. Families suffered, and buildings, homes, railways, and bridges were destroyed. It was a long, horrible war.

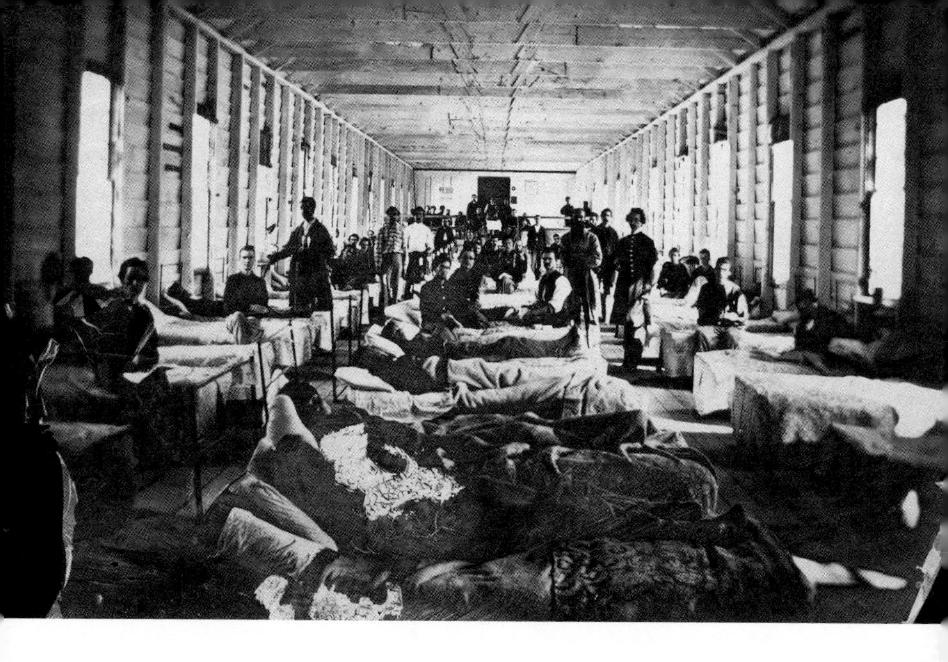

Clara could not even apply to join the Union Army, though. “A woman’s place is in the home,” an officer told her. Clara was angry and disappointed that the officer would hinder her choice to be a soldier.

Clara did some research and came up with a new plan. She knew the army did not have enough supplies for the troops. Clara would get the supplies the army needed. Other women heard about her work, and they sent supplies to Clara. She would bring the supplies to the soldiers in hospitals and camps.

Gettysburg National Military Park

Clara on the Battlefield

This was right where Clara Barton wanted to be: on the battlefields of the Civil War. When Clara arrived on the battlefield, it was an awful scene. There were many injured soldiers, and bullets flew through the air.

In the middle of it all was Clara, in her bonnet with a red bow around her neck. The only thing she cared about at that moment was helping the injured soldiers.

A wounded soldier, lying on his back, called out, "Please give me water!" Clara ran to him with a cup and lifted his head to give him a drink. Just then, a bullet ripped through the sleeve of her shirt. Clara looked at the hole the bullet had made and realized she was lucky to be alive. Even in danger, Clara never stopped helping the soldiers. She gave the soldier his drink and then left to help others in need.

In a battle near Antietam Creek in Maryland, the Union army would need Clara's help. The famous Robert E. Lee had his Confederate army there. George McClellan led the Union troops, and Clara was with the Union soldiers. The battle was taking place in fields near the creek.

Clara and her small crew got into her supply wagon and rode toward the fighting. They stopped at an old barn where there were many injured soldiers waiting for help. "This is where we are needed," Clara said.

A Hidden Hospital

Clara unloaded the wagon as more wounded soldiers came to the barn. She and her crew were so close to the battle that she could see the Union cannons.

Clara couldn't find any doctors at the barn. Then she found out why. Her wagon driver had found a farmhouse nearby. It was difficult to see because it was built in a low area. The driver told Clara that the doctors were at the farmhouse, so Clara quickly gathered up some bandages and ran there.

Dr. James Dunn was standing in the doorway. He led Clara to a wounded soldier, whose wounds were covered with cornhusks. This was a clever invention, but bandages would work better! Clara pulled out her bandages and wrapped the wound.

Dr. Dunn was thrilled that Clara was there to help him. He was also relieved that she had so many medical supplies. Clara began to treat other wounds. She gave the soldiers water and offered them kind words.

The fierce battle continued. There were many explosions. The top floor of the farmhouse was full of holes because so many bullets had hit it.

Clara continued to work. She ran back and forth between the barn and the farmhouse. More and more injured soldiers arrived. Many had bad wounds and were in pain. It was a horrible situation. Clara did her best to ease their suffering.

By the early afternoon, Clara was running out of food. She looked in the farmhouse cellar and found a bag of cornmeal there. She added water to it and made a thin mixture called *gruel.*

Some of the many injured soldiers were southern soldiers who had been captured. Clara fed them, too. As she spooned out gruel to them, they said, "Thank you." They appreciated that the woman from the North was so kind to them.

The battle ended late in the afternoon with neither side winning. Thousands of soldiers from both sides lost their lives.

The sun went down on the battlefield, but Clara Barton had more work to do. Many injured soldiers still needed help. One doctor was upset because his last candle was almost gone. Clara fetched a box of lanterns from her supplies, and the doctor was thrilled. With her help, he worked through the night.

Clara helped the Civil War soldiers for three years. Then, since many other volunteers had come to help, she decided it was time to return home.

Clara Barton later became the first president of the American Red Cross. The Red Cross is a volunteer group that helps people in trouble all over the world.

Clara Barton lived a long and very busy life. She died on April 12, 1912. Even though she did many other important things in her life, she was always known as "The Angel of the Battlefield."

Think Critically

1. How would you describe Clara Barton?
2. Why wasn't Clara Barton allowed to join the Union Army?
3. What job did Clara have before she went to the battlefield?
4. Why do you think Clara Barton gave food to enemy soldiers?
5. How did reading about Clara Barton working on the battlefield make you feel?

Science

Look it Up Clara Barton worked as a nurse to help the injured soldiers. Find out what nurses do today and make a list of the things that interest you.

School-Home Connection Tell a family member what you learned about Clara Barton. Then have a discussion about people you know who help other people.

Word Count: 989 (993)